T0016122

Also available in this series from Quadrille:

MINDFULNESS
MINDFULNESS II
QUIET
FRIENDSHIP
LOVE
CONFIDENCE
TIDINESS
HAPPINESS
MOTHERHOOD
LUCK
US
SEX
CHRISTMAS
SISTERHOOD
SELF-CARE
KINDNESS
BRIDESMAIDS
PRIDE
GRATITUDE
POSITIVITY
UNITY
HOPE

the little book of SELF-LOVE

Hardie Grant
QUADRILLE

Self-love

Definition:

verb

Regard for one's own wellbeing and happiness.

Self-love is an essential action that allows you to properly observe, care for and love your body, mind and soul, which will in turn help you to fully and properly love others.

Understanding you are worthy of your own love is the first step to unrolling the love within your heart to others.

Three self-love mantras to use at daybreak

1. As the light brightens my world, I am deserving of its warmth.
2. Today I shall choose to love myself as I love others.
3. A new day comes and I shall accept its gifts.

"If you love yourself, you love everybody else as you do yourself. As long as you love another person less than you love yourself, you will not really succeed in loving yourself but if you love all alike, including yourself, you will love them as one person."

MEISTER ECKHART

Play the hate/love swapsies game

Think about the parts of your body or personality that you have historically found difficult to love. Think carefully and honestly about why you hate them and consider if your reasoning is exaggerated, and if you can find a way to show gratitude instead. Gently turn away from your negative responses and look upon those troublesome areas with compassion and love. There will be reasons to swap hate for love if you only allow yourself to look with a loving heart.

I hate how hairy my legs get...
I am grateful that my legs enable me
to do activities that I love.

I hate blushing...
I love the emotional honesty of
my response.

I hate being a nervous flyer...
I love that I am resilient enough
to travel the world anyway.

Self-love idea

Curate the first moments of your day so that you wake with love, not with a grumble or in a rush. Make the first moment of the day your own.

- If you need to wake up early, choose a beautiful tune for your alarm, or sleep with the curtains open to wake with the rising sun.
- Savour five minutes alone before you share your day with others. Leave the bedroom to meditate or enjoy a hot drink in complete peace.
- Use the most luxurious soaps and shampoos you can afford so that your morning cleanse is a daily treat, not a chore.

Self-love gives you permission to dream big... Business owner? Holiday of a lifetime? True love? A gold sequined dress? It's all within your grasp... Self-love does not set a limit on your dreams; instead, it tells you that you are worthy of them coming true.

The science of self-love

In 2008, researchers at the University of Wisconsin proved the cognitive power of self-love by using MRI imagery while volunteers practised loving-kindness-compassion meditations. They discovered that the more self-compassion people displayed, the greater the range of emotional tools they had to rely on.

Similarly, the power of self-forgiveness was revealed in a study published in 2010, in *The Official Journal of the International Society for the Study of*

Individual Differences. 119 students were surveyed: all were studying at Carleton University and all had procrastinated about revising for their exams. The study found that those who forgave themselves for their earlier procrastination were better able to avoid procrastinating in future.

Allocate time and space to consider what is holding you back from loving yourself. Identify the strongest barriers and test them. For example, does your upbringing seem to dictate your present mindset? Or do you put self-care and self-love on the backburner in favour of work or family duties?

Spend some time figuring these out, then ask yourself what you can do to overcome them and make self-love a non-negotiable part of your life.

Journal prompts to identify barriers to self-love

1. What's stopping me from practising self-love?
2. How can I break these patterns?
3. What can I start doing *right now* to love myself more?

Imagine living in a world where everyone hated themselves – in the workplace, in a flatshare, the strangers on the street. It would be a NIGHTMARE!

Self-love is essential not only for the benefit on the one doing the self-loving, but for all those who share their space.

She who loves herself does not wait to be treated to a fancy meal.

She who loves herself will assemble the ingredients herself and feed her own soul – not just with food, but with nourishing ideas and loving thoughts, too.

Who do you wake up with?

Who do you take a shower with?

Who do you walk to work with?

Who do you drink too many cups of coffee with?

Who do you spend 24 hours of the day with?

If the answer to any of the above is YOU, you better get on with loving that person – you sure do hang out a lot together!

*"Self-love, the spring of motion, acts the soul;
Reason's comparing balance rules the whole."*

ALEXANDER POPE

In this beautiful couplet Alexander Pope calls self-love the 'spring of motion'. This is a delightful idea, that self-love is needed to inspire the soul to movement. Think of the new born baby seeking mother's milk. It is the self-love instinct that stirs the child to life.

"True friendship is self-love at second hand; where, as in a flattering mirror we may see our virtues magnified and our errors softened, and where we may fancy our opinion of ourselves confirmed by an impartial and faithful witness."

WILLIAM HAZLITT

Three benefits of friendship when self-love reigns supreme

1. When you love yourself into building a strong emotional foundation, you have the capacity to offer nurturing support to your friends.

2. You are able to model self-love and share the benefits of feeling happy in your own skin, leading to happier, healthier friends.

3. If self-love is already in the bag, you'll spend less time on mutual reassurance and more time on having fun!

"One cannot reflect in streaming water. Only those who know internal peace can give it to others."

LAOZI

It is often said that people tend to overvalue what they are not, and undervalue what they are. Consider this carefully when viewing yourself. Rather than focussing on what you are *not*, in terms of looks, status or finance for example, celebrate what you *are*. Write a list. . .

I am. . . educated.

I am. . . healthy.

I am. . . loyal.

You are always more than you initially realize.

At the core of your attitude and mindset is your view of yourself. When introspecting, show yourself compassion and tenderness. Use kind and positive language when contemplating who you are.

Write a character description of yourself

Step into the shoes of a casting director and pen a detailed brief about you as if you are the star of your favourite genre movie. Remember: only use positive, kind words.

Self-love means creating a consistent picture of your life, in which all parts of you – your daily rituals, self-care regime, career aspirations, relationships and more – weave together to make a coherent whole that's brimming with self-compassion.

Once you've developed a cohesive set of behaviours, goals and beliefs, keep checking in with yourself to ensure all aspects of your life are in sync. If they are not, consider what can be done to lean back into the loving image you have created of yourself.

In the quiet moments of the day take the time to thank yourself. Thank your body for working, thank your mind for thinking, thank your soul for feeling.

Five self-love gratitude mantras

1. I thank today for the light and life it brings me.
2. I thank myself for the possibilities I bring to this world.
3. I thank my body for the life it allows me.
4. I thank my mind and its connection with the universe.
5. I thank my spirit for moving me to succeed today.

Curate a list of small, loving moments to appreciate

1. Make a list of aspects of your daily routine that you already love: watering your balcony box or savouring your evening aperitif, for example.
2. Ensure that every time you engage with this task, you take a moment to thoroughly appreciate it.
3. If the activity involves someone else, take a moment to tell them how much pleasure it brings you.
4. Consider ways of embellishing and expanding upon these scenes of joy – why not invest in a snazzy new watering can or a pair of crystal glasses to drink from?

“I am a man of simple pleasures. The best suits me perfectly.”

OSCAR WILDE

Imagine you are taking care of a loved one. Ask yourself. . .

1. What would you feed them?
2. How would you clothe them?
3. How would you keep them fit and healthy?
4. How would you educate them?
5. How would you entertain them?
6. Where in the world would you like them to visit?
7. What experiences must they enjoy?

Now, extend that same loving attitude towards yourself. Viewing yourself as if you are one of your loved ones helps to emphasize that you, like them, are in need of nuturing. It shows how precious you are, and that you deserve love, compassion and care, too.

Self-love nurtures the soul by. . .

Loving deeply.

Exploring the infinite unknown.

Finding meaning and purpose.

Self-love nurtures the mind by...

Remaining curious.

Trying new experiences.

Learning new skills.

Self-love nurtures the whole self by. . .

Forming solid relationships.

Maintaining offline connections.

Finding joy in the everyday.

Self-love: the basics

- One functioning bra is not quite enough.
- Ditto: that one pair of tights without ladders.
- Ditto: only four pairs of knickers.
- Ditto: a jumble of odd socks.

Self-love allows you to invest in the prettiest and highest quality items you wear close to your skin every day. If in doubt about a dubious piece of underwear, ask yourself if you would be happy giving it to your best friend? If not, why is it good enough for you?

"Self-respect is the noblest garment with which a man can clothe himself, the most elevating feeling with which the mind can be inspired."

SAMUEL SMILES

Self-love: the essential appointments never to be avoided!

- Regular visits to the dental hygienist.
- The doctor (even if you think it's nothing).
- The car mechanic – it's carrying around a precious object and needs to be in tip-top condition.
- The gym (schedule it like a work appointment to make it part of your routine).
- Date night with your lover.

"There is only one corner of the universe that you can be certain of improving and that's your own self."

ALDOUS HUXLEY

"Friendship with oneself is important, because without it one cannot be friends with anyone else in the world."

ELEANOR ROOSEVELT

Follow up self-love affirmations with a reminder to act on them

'I am compassionate.'

Be kind to all you meet.

'I am competent.'

Take care to finish tasks you begin.

'I am beautiful.'

Practise a healthy relationship with fitness and nutrition.

"The soul is dyed the colour of its thoughts. Think only on those things that are in line with your principles and can bear the light of day. The content of your character is your choice. Day by day, what you choose, what you think, and what you do is who you become. Your integrity is your destiny... it is the light that guides your way."

HERACLITUS

"It's your life – but only if you make it so. The standards by which you live must be your own standards, your own values, your own convictions in regard to what is right and wrong, what is true and false, what is important and what is trivial. When you adopt the standards and the values of someone else . . . you surrender your own integrity. You become, to the extent of your surrender, less of a human being."

ELEANOR ROOSEVELT

Amour propre is the French term for self-love and self-esteem. Championed by the philosopher Jean Jacques Rousseau, *amour propre* translates as a belief and confidence in your own ability and value.

"Why should we build our happiness on the opinion of others, when we can find it in our own hearts?"

JEAN-JACQUES ROUSSEAU

Self-love thought experiment

1. How much do you think you're worth?
2. How much does your family think you're worth?
3. How much does your employer think you're worth?
4. How much does your community think you're worth?
5. Is there alignment in the differing values placed on you?
6. Do you recognize the value placed on you by others?

The Ancient Greeks fully understood the concept of self-love and devised the word *philautia* from *philos* (love) and *autos* (oneself). *Philautia* is divided into two aspects, one where self-love is negative and associated with selfishness and vanity, and the other more positive understanding where *philautia* is concerned with self-compassion and self-respect.

Consider the word *philautia* the next time a part of you is hurting. Let's imagine you have a shoulder that is stiff or an ankle that is recovering from injury. Our first response is often annoyance and we send angry thoughts to our misbehaving body parts. 'I hate my neck/elbow/thighs,' we shout crossly. Instead, treat our sore or injured body parts with compassion and speak kindly to them. Think of *philautia* and speak gently, with tender loving words.

Embrace the Greek concept of *meraki*. Almost untranslatable, the term refers to the idea of leaving part of yourself in everything you do. Similar to 'throwing yourself into something', *meraki* speaks to the passion and energy and wholehearted concentration you dedicate to tasks.

Consider the concept of *meraki* when baking, writing, cleaning, dressing, gifting or presenting. Choose to embed part of yourself within these tasks. When you are brimming with self-love there is extra love to work with. Think of *meraki* a little like self-love fairy dust and leave a sprinkling of yourself in all that you do.

Why not celebrate the concept of *atma-prema*, the ancient Sanskrit term for unconditional self-love? Understanding the Eastern concept of the divine force living in all people helps to impress the importance of giving yourself due deference. There is divine force within all souls (including yours) and as such, you must be honoured.

Six *atma-prema* mantras

1. I am divine love.
2. Love lives in me.
3. My soul is divine.
4. I am part of the divine oneness.
5. My nature is divine.
6. I love my soul as I love the universe.

"You yourself are even another little world and have within you the sun and the moon and also the stars."

ORIGEN

“Carpe diem! *Rejoice while you are alive; enjoy the day; live life to the fullest; make the most of what you have. It is later than you think.*”

HORACE

Embrace the Italian concept of *bella figura*. Translated literally as 'the beautiful figure', *bella figura* alludes generally to making a good impression, a fine appearance. And don't the Italians just do this! The Italians know how to make love to the self by feeding it delicious food, clothing it exquisitely and driving it around in the most stylish of motors. As one of the most self-confident nationalities, the Italians know just how to make every aspect of life as elegant as can be.

Ciao bella!

How to self-love like the Italians

1. Eat good homecooked food with relish.
2. Seek out beautiful buildings and countryside.
3. Dress well, for you are a person of beauty.
4. Express your passions and emotions.
5. Keep family at the heart of everything.

‘Mens sana in corpore sano.’

‘A healthy mind in a healthy body.’

This famous quote by Juvenal speaks to the twin pillars that are necessary for a balanced life. Consider using the quote as a self-love mantra to remind yourself that both aspects of yourself need care and attention.

Three ways to celebrate National Self-Love Day on 13 February

1. Treat yourself to a new self-pleasuring device.
2. Cook yourself a perfect dinner for one – consisting entirely of what you fancy.
3. Watch the sunset alone reflecting on who you are.

Self-love challenges to set yourself

- Say no to something once a week.
- Say yes to something once a week.
- Arrange a night out.
- Arrange a night in.
- Call a friend.
- Quietly uncouple from a toxic friend.

Self-love lists to journal

- 5 things you love about your home.
- 4 things you love about your body.
- 3 things about your career you'd like to improve.
- 2 things about your fitness you'd like to improve.
- 1 thing about your relationship you'd like to improve.

(Self-love tip: as you list, make sure you're focussing on positives, whether that's things you're grateful for or future goals. Avoid dwelling on the negatives!)

On cold nights, self-love loves...

Sheepskin bootie slippers.

Merino dressing gowns.

Warm cocoa.

Open fires.

Faux fur throws.

Silk pillowcases.

That feeling of warm contentment.

On hot summer days, self-love loves. . .

Rosewater facial spritz.

Diamante flip flops.

Argan hair oil.

Organic cotton dresses.

Cucumber and mint water.

That feeling of hot summer promise.

Three self-love mantras

1. I am the best me there is.
2. I love who I am.
3. I deserve the best.

“We ourselves possess Beauty when we are true to our own being; ugliness is in going over to another order; knowing ourselves, we are beautiful; in self-ignorance we are ugly.”

PLOTINUS

"Go back inside yourself and look: if you do not yet see yourself as beautiful [this refers to the beauty of the soul rather than physical beauty], then do as the sculptor does with a statue he wants to make beautiful; he chisels away one part, and levels off another, makes one spot smooth and another clear, until he shows forth a beautiful face on the statue.

Like him, remove what is superfluous, straighten what is crooked, clean up what is dark and make it bright, and never stop sculpting your own statue, until the godlike splendour of virtue shines forth to you…"

PLOTINUS

Ask yourself the question: how would I practise self-love if I had endless time and resources?

A daily massage? A monthly mini break? A sabbatical?

Articulating our self-love dreams is the first step to fulfilling them. While they may not all immediately materialize, you may succeed in identifying one or two desires that can be actualized. Look carefully and honestly at your self-love dreams and see what you can incorporate into your current life. A massage could be self-administered, a mini break booked and a sabbatical discussed with your manager.

Self-love acknowledges that happiness is not a luxury, pleasure is not a crime and ambition is something to embrace with pride.

To improve low self-esteem, the UK's NHS recommends. . .

- Recognizing what you're good at.
- Building positive relationships.
- Being kind to yourself.
- Learning to be assertive.
- Starting to say no.
- Challenging yourself.

"The greatest evil that can befall man is that he should come to think ill of himself."

JOHANN WOLFGANG VON GOETHE

Self-love does not seek to draw a veil over our faults, but rather to approach our faults with the same loving kindness and generosity that we would others.

Self-love teaches you to. . .

- Admire the beauty of others without doubting your own.
- Celebrate the achievements of others without criticizing yourself.
- Share in someone else's romantic journey without bewailing your own relationship status.

Self-love as a daily practice

One bubble bath does not a self-love goddess make! For self-love to work its magic, it must become a way of life, something that is done every day without thinking. The self-confident smile in the mirror, the nutritious lunch with a friend, the half an hour spent reading a novel before bed. Self-love is an attitude that accepts you must spend consistent time and effort looking after yourself, every day, in order to find the self-fulfilment necessary for a flourishing life.

Meet the 13th century Sufi mystic poet Jalāl al-Dīn Muhammad Rūmī. His writings are some of the most exquisite on all matters of love and the heart. He writes of the divine connection between two people, between earth and heaven and within one's own soul.

Light a candle, curl up on your sofa or beneath your favourite tree and immerse yourself in Rūmī's words about the importance of surrounding yourself in love.

"Your task is not to seek love, but merely to seek and find all the barriers within yourself that you have built against it."

RŪMĪ

"Lose yourself,
Lose yourself in this Love.
When you lose yourself in this Love,
you will find everything.

Lose yourself,
Lose yourself.
Do not fear this loss,
for you will rise from the earth
and embrace the endless heavens.

Lose yourself,
Lose yourself.
Escape from the black cloud
that surrounds you.
Then you will see your own light
as radiant as the full moon.

Now enter that silence.
This is the surest way
to lose yourself...

What is your life about anyway?
Nothing but a struggle to be someone.
Nothing but a running from your
own silence.

Who said the eternal one has died?
Who said the light of hope has died?
The enemy of the Sun is on the rooftop.
With his eyes closed he yells out,
'The brilliant Sun has died!'"

RŪMĪ

"You give yourself a kiss. If you want to hold the beautiful one, hold yourself."

RŪMĪ

Create a self-love meditation

Learn a Rūmī poem off by heart and base a self-love meditation on the repetition of his entrancing words.

Loving yourself despite your flaws helps you to become a more compassionate friend, lover and colleague. Practising self-love while accepting your flaws embeds in you the notion that flaws are human and that everyone – especially you – is deserving of love and understanding.

If we look for criticism we will find it.

If we look for complaint we will hear it.

If we look for doubt we will stumble across it.

Look instead for love, for harmony and for understanding. If we look with an open heart within and without, we will find love, harmony and understanding.

"Everything that irritates us about others can lead us to an understanding of ourselves."

CARL JUNG

Write an 'Irritating List'

Write a list of things you find most irritating about other people. Overlay this list with some aspects of your own character you would like to work on. Seeing irritation as outsiders do can speed up change within ourselves. Go easy though – remember this is a self-love exercise!

"Be careful whom you associate with. It is human to imitate the habits of those with whom we interact. We inadvertently adopt their interests, their opinions, their values, and their habit of interpreting events... The key is to keep company only with people who uplift you, whose presence calls forth your best."

EPICTETUS

Avoid people who. . .

Put you down.

Take advantage of you.

Undermine your accomplishments.

Have a default negative setting.

Nurture friends who. . .

Are happy to see you.

Cheer you on.

Don't compete with you.

Listen without judgement.

Abandon the idea that there is one self. We are all many people to many different people at different stages of our lives. We are not the same at 80 as we were at eight. We are different on the sofa with our lover than in the boardroom with our boss. While we all have an intrinsic self, it is malleable and each different facet of our character requires different levels of self-love.

Compile a list of your different 'selves' and consider whether they are all receiving the necessary love.

Work self.

Home self.

Friend self.

Fitness self.

Community self.

Family self.

Alone self.

Sociable self.

"I am large, I contain multitudes."

WALT WHITMAN

Self-love does not tolerate. . .

Rudeness.

Bad manners.

Deliberate oversight.

Temper tantrums.

Guilt-tripping.

Gossiping.

Coercion.

Being regularly late.

Self-love says...

'No. Please do not treat me like this. I deserve better.'

"I always deserve the best treatment because I never put up with any other."

JANE AUSTEN
from *Emma*

Self-love belongs in the workplace

Self-love – the idea that you are worthy of respect and dignity – is an empowering force within the workplace. Whether you're facing issues of passive aggressive behaviour or outright discrimination, self-love in the workplace enables you to address issues armed with the belief that your integrity demands it.

“Both our first and last love is self-love.”

CHRISTIAN BOVEE

Self-love helps us to relax in our own company within a variety of environments. The roomful of strangers, the large family gathering or the parents at the school gate can all present challenges, when we feel we are not quite our authentic selves.

Self-love questions to ask before entering uncomfortable situations

1. Do I *have* to be here?
2. Do I *want* to be here?
3. What am I worried about?

Self-love mantras to repeat before entering uncomfortable situations

1. I choose to be here.
2. I choose to be myself here.
3. I choose to leave when I am ready.

Self-love recognizes that we are entitled to be our authentic selves within all our relationships. Consider who you are to different people: daughter, sister, mother, lover, wife, colleague, neighbour, leader, team player. Loving yourself within all these relationships helps them all to grow in strength and quality.

Identify your different selves

From your 'exercise-bunny self' to your 'spiritual-seeking self', all of us encompass many selves. List all of your different selves and identify how best you can serve them. Would 'exercise-bunny self' enjoy a revved up workout with a friend, and 'spiritual-seeking self' appreciate joining a community prayer meeting, for example? Indulge all your different selves as part of a holistic self-love package.

"Be steady and well-ordered in your life so that you can be fierce and original in your work."

GUSTAVE FLAUBERT

Self-love asks if what you are doing today is getting you closer to where you want to be tomorrow.

Identify moments in your day when self-love is most needed

Whether rushing for the bus or sugar crashing in the afternoon, there are moments in every day when we are not our best selves. Identify these moment and deploy self-love accurately.

- Observe your daily routine to identify patterns and pinch points.
- After establishing the lows, ask why they are happening.
- Consider changing your routine, with new timetabling or rearranged dietary habits.
- Present kind and positive solutions as you would to a dear friend.

"Human behaviour flows from three main sources: desire, emotion and knowledge."

PLATO

Ask yourself. . .

What is my *desire* for self-love?

What are my *emotions* around self-love?

What *knowledge* do I need to acquire to support self-love?

Self-love understands that you won't make others happy by making yourself sad.

Self-love recognizes our dependence on others. In the same way that parents can only ever be as happy as their unhappiest child, our personal flourishing is dependent on the thriving of our closest family and friends. When practising self-love, there is room to support others and to care for others in times of crisis and pain.

At some point all of us whisper to ourselves or our loved one, 'I've lost who I am.' Our true selves have become smothered in work or family commitments and we have entirely forgotten who we love to be.

3 ways of recovering your lost self

1. Find a photograph from when you were happiest and glowing with energy. Use it as your screen saver as a constant reminder of the energy you'd like to channel again.

2. Compile a list of obstacles to finding yourself again. Sit with the explanations and consider what can be done.

3. Allocate time every week, even it is just an hour, to either inhabit your lost self, or create concrete plans on how to reintegrate this lost self into your current life.

When the light is returning, use self-love to. . .

- Give yourself permission to enjoy life again.
- Choose your favourite daily routines to re-establish.
- Forgive yourself if you retreat into sadness.
- Gift yourself items and experience that will bring joy.

"Be happy for this moment. This moment is your life."

OMAR KHAYYAM

"The duty we owe ourselves is greater than that we owe others."

LOUISA MAY ALCOTT

Just as we would encourage a child to share their new skill or show their beautiful piece of work, self-love helps give us the confidence to share our talents with the world.

"Some people go through life trying to find out what the world holds for them only to find out too late that it's what they bring to the world that really counts."

LUCY MAUD MONTGOMERY

"If you want to ignite others must first burn inside yourself."

CHARLOTTE BRONTË

Create opportunities for personal development

- Learn a new skill: expanding your repertoire of skills will help you feel accomplished and remind you how brilliant you are.
- Invest time and resources in a hobby: you deserve to enjoy your skills and talents on a regular basis.
- Set yourself a challenge (and complete it): accomplishing a challenge, no matter how small, immediately boosts feelings of self-worth.

"A man of character finds a special attractiveness in difficulty, since it is only by coming to grips with difficulty that he can realize his or her potentialities."

CHARLES DE GAULLE

Self-love tips for people pleasers

- Avoid berating yourself for being a people pleaser – at a basic level, serving others is a noble personality trait (so long as it does not come at a cost to you)!
- Establish a self-esteem maintenance programme (meditation, affirmations, socializing – whatever works for you) and stick to it.
- Consciously consider goals that you have set for yourself and only you can achieve, thereby associating success with your desire rather than the responses of others.
- Constantly ask yourself: am I doing this for others or for me?

Self-love tips for indecisive people

- Can't make up your mind if this is you? Read on... and relax, it's good to be thoughtful.
- Give yourself permission to practise self-love.
- Practise saying YES to things you love to do even if they seem complicated.
- Develop micro self-love rituals that require little pre-planning or forethought (keep a luxurious hand-cream in your day bag or emergency sweets in the glove compartment, for example).

Self-love tips for extroverts

- Use your buzzing communication skills to seek self-love ideas from other people. Learning how your neighbour goes sea-swimming every Monday for example can help expand your self-love repertoire.
- Start conversations about self-love within your community and help people who may need a little more loving kindness in their daily lives.
- Finding time in quietude will help to recharge your batteries for the next circuit of fun and friends.

Self-love tips for introverts

- Don't worry – you only need to tell people about your self-love journey if you are comfortable with sharing.
- Use your watchful nature to carefully observe what makes you glow with pleasure. Choose to spend more time on these pleasurable activities.
- Refuse to listen to the whispers of self-doubt that creep about – silence them instead with positive affirmations.
- Create a pact with yourself about how you intend to treat yourself.

Self-love recognizes that nurturing of the mind, body and soul are not luxuries but essential to a life well lived.

"No gift will ever buy back a man's love when you have removed his self-love."

JOHN STEINBECK

"Be yourself, everyone else is taken."

OSCAR WILDE

"Once we know ourselves, we may learn how to care for ourselves – but otherwise we never shall."

SOCRATES

The golden rule of self-love: put yourself first!

By elevating yourself in your list of priorities you are acknowledging your self-worth, self-value and self-responsibility both to yourself and to others.

If you won't put yourself first
– who will?

"Nine requisites for contented living: Health enough to make work a pleasure.

Wealth enough to support your needs.

Strength to battle with difficulties and overcome them.

Grace enough to confess your sins and forsake them.

Patience enough to toil until some good is accomplished.

Charity enough to see some good in your neighbour.

Love enough to move you to be useful and helpful to others.

Faith enough to make real the things of God.

Hope enough to remove all anxious fears concerning the future.”

JOHANN WOLFGANG VON GOETHE
‘Nine Requisites for Contented Living’

Self-love challenge

Do you agree with German genius Johann Wolfgang von Goethe on the 'Nine Requisites for a Contented Life'? Consider writing your own list of the essentials that you require to lead your perfectly contented life.

Create a figurative compliment bouquet

Whenever you receive a compliment treat it like a flower and assemble a compliment bouquet at the end of the week. Treat yourself to a bouquet of real fresh flowers and remember the compliments of each individual bloom.

Self-love recognizes the importance of doing something you're good at

As Einstein famously said, 'If you judge a fish by its ability to climb a tree, it will live its whole life believing it is stupid.' Self-love recognizes the necessity of working to your strengths, rather than constantly fighting your weaknesses.

- Establish what you are good at (ask friends and colleagues if unsure).
- Overlay your daily life with your skill set – do they tally?
- If you are not doing what you are good at on a daily basis, be open to reconsidering working and family arrangements to make better use of your craft and expertise.

"We are always more anxious to be distinguished for a talent which we do not possess, than to be praised for the fifteen which we do possess."

MARK TWAIN

Self-love is acutely relevant during dark times. Just ask the wise men and women who navigated internal and external misery.

How to self-love when deeply wounded

At times of overwhelming grief and despairing heartache, self-love can act as a tender lifeline. With the support of professional help where necessary, self-love, when despondent and heartsore, is a tender and vital act.

- Give yourself time and tenderness.
- Share your emotional condition with someone who you trust.
- Understand that heartache and despair after tragedy are natural human responses.
- Nourish yourself with essential food, water and sleep as you would care for an injured animal.

"A wound in the soul, coming from the rending of the spiritual body, strange as it may seem, gradually closes like a physical wound. And once a deep wound heals over and the edges seem to have knit, a wound in the soul, like a physical wound, can be healed only by the force of life pushing up from inside. This was the way Natasha's wound healed. She thought her life was over. But suddenly her love for her mother showed her that the essence of life – love – was still alive in her. Love awoke, and life awoke."

LEO TOLSTOY
War and Peace

This passage from Tolstoy's *War and Peace* describes Natasha Rostova's recovery from a bout of heartbreak and depression through love and the 'essence of life'.

How to self-love after a setback

After a career or romantic setback self-love can entirely desert us. We fall back into the pernicious arms of self-loathing and self-pity. It is imperative at times like this to speak to ourselves as we would speak to our best beloved suffering a similar setback. We would soothe, sympathize, encourage and plan ahead. Step outside the emotion and look upon your wounded self with the compassion you would naturally give to others.

The three Ps of self-love after a setback

1. Pause: give yourself time to lick your wounds.
2. Patience: if you need another duvet day, have one.
3. Plan: ask yourself what you need to move forward – and take it.

Mediation inhalation and exhalation mantras

Inhale: I am worthy.

Exhale: I am grateful.

Inhale: I am loved.

Exhale: I love.

Inhale: I am myself.

Exhale: I am enough.

Inhale: I love myself.
Exhale: I deserve this love.

Inhale: I give myself peace.
Exhale: I accept this peace.

Inhale: I bless myself.
Exhale: I am blessed.

Adopt a self-love position when meditating. Place one of your hands gently on your forehead or at your heart to help channel your energy back into yourself.

"Keep away from those who try to belittle your ambitions. Small people always do that, but the really great make you believe that you too can become great."

MARK TWAIN

The 10 second daily self-love challenge

There are some days when we haven't the bandwidth for candle filled self-love sessions. Life is too frenetic and there are needs other than our own that need tending. Try out these 10 second self-love mantras to programme your mind towards self-love, no matter how full the day.

1. Find stillness and peace for 10 seconds.
2. Close your eyes and breathe deeply and slowly.
3. Hold one thought in your mind for 10 seconds.

A week of self-love mantras

Monday: Today I shall not take to heart the opinions of others.

Tuesday: Today I shall not compare myself unfavourably to others.

Wednesday: Today I shall allow myself to make mistakes.

Thursday: Today I shall trust myself.

Friday: Today I shall be grateful for my body carrying me through the day.

Saturday: Today I shall allow myself to have fun.

Sunday: Today I shall acknowledge all of the good things I endeavour to do.

Struggling to fully embrace self-love? Imagine you are a much honoured visitor and treat yourself accordingly. Have you been brought up to put others before you? Does self-love not come naturally? If this is the case, imagine you are an honoured guest staying for a while. When choosing your imaginary guest, pick someone you care deeply about – a family member or role model. Jot down a few things that you would organize for their stay including creature comforts and entertainment. Apply these same ideas to you and treat yourself as you would your honoured guest.

Ideas for the 'honoured guest' (AKA you!)

- Clean sheets (even when it's not the usual wash day).
- A vase of flowers by the bed.
- Hot cocoa and a good soak before sleep.

Conduct a self-love audit

In the blizzard of work and family commitments, we lose sight of what we really love. By conducting a self-love audit we can tune back in to elements of life that make our heart sing. If you find it uncomfortable assessing your life, imagine you are conducting a self-love audit on a dear friend. See yourself in the third person to help reduce the sticky bits.

"When we are no longer able to change a situation – we are challenged to change ourselves."

VICTOR FRANKL

Four steps to reassess your self-love

1. Divide your life into easily manageable segments: family, romance, home, finances, work, leisure, spirituality, fitness, community.
2. For each section ask yourself: Am I happy? Where would I like to improve? What can I do to make this area of my life flourish? Who can help me with this?
3. Track the amount of time and energy you are giving to each area of your life. If one aspect is heavily weighted and another in receipt

of little attention, work out ways of creating an equilibrium.

4. Set yourself small goals to embellish those areas of life that need particular care and attention. Ask friends and family for help.

Remember:

Self-love is not a solitary affair.

"What does love look like? It has the hands to help others. It has the feet to hasten to the poor and needy. It has eyes to see misery and want. It has the ears to hear the sighs and sorrows of men. That is what love looks like."

SAINT AUGUSTINE

Self-love means inviting others to participate in your life in positive and appropriate ways. Just as you wouldn't take your car to a doctor to be fixed, ensure you allocate the right people to care for all aspects of your health and wellbeing. Consider how your relationships with different people are meaningful in different ways, and how they each support your self-love journey.

'Self-love support staff' checklist

- Career mentor
- Health caregivers for regular check-ups
- Friends for socializing
- Friends for emotional support
- Therapist for the really tricky problems
- Accountant and financial advisor
- Two people to call in an emergency
- A hairdresser you trust
- Fitness buddy

Don't be bashful – the pleasure that others will receive in helping you is real and meaningful and will benefit them just as much as it benefits you.

While suffering with depression, the popular Victorian poet Gerard Manley Hopkins invites his own heart to have more pity on his own self. 'My Own Heart Let Me Have Pity on. . .' is a poem to cherish when dark feelings descend, to remind yourself to be kind to your own heart.

"My own heart let me more have pity on; let
Me live to my sad self hereafter kind,
Charitable; not live this tormented mind
With this tormented mind tormenting yet.
I cast for comfort I can no more get
By groping round my comfortless, than blind
Eyes in their dark can day or thirst can find
Thirst's all-in-all in all a world of wet.

Soul, self; come, poor Jackself,
I do advise
You, jaded, let be; call off
thoughts awhile
Elsewhere; leave comfort root-room;
let joy size
At God knows when to God knows
what; whose smile
's not wrung, see you; unforeseen times
rather – as skies
Betweenpie mountains – lights
a lovely mile."

GERARD MANLEY HOPKINS

Self-forgiveness is key to successful self-loving. By disentangling your past mistakes from your present self, you are better able to feel worthy of self-love.

Five ways to self-forgive

1. To err is human; understand that everyone makes mistakes.
2. Contemplate your mistake and fully appreciate how it has affected you and others.
3. Ask for forgiveness, of others if necessary and chiefly yourself.
4. Grant yourself forgiveness.
5. Give yourself permission to move on.

Three self-forgiveness rituals

1. Write yourself a letter explaining how you hurt yourself and perhaps others. Ask yourself for forgiveness. Respond with a forgiving letter absolving yourself of the wrong and giving yourself permission to live freely in the light of forgiveness.

2. Actively seek to make amends. Accompany your self-forgiveness with a positive (not punishing) act, volunteering at the local youth group, for example. Completing an altruistic act will help you feel you deserve your self-forgiveness.

"The more you know yourself, the more you forgive yourself."

CONFUCIUS

"The weak can never forgive. Forgiveness is the hallmark of the strong."

MAHATMA GANDHI

Who benefits from me *not* loving myself?

If lack of self-love goes unaddressed for too long, you can bet anything that someone, somewhere, will be benefiting. Working out who these people are helps to motivate us into seeing our lack of self-love clearly, and to do something about it. For example, your finances are in a mess. Realizing that the banks or the insurers are taking more from you than they require is a great motivating factor in finally getting round to ordering your accounts.

Ask yourself: Who benefits from my lack of self-love in relation to. . .

Money? Food? Fashion? Alcohol? Demanding colleagues? Work/life balance?

If the answer is not ME, then consider what can be done to rebalance the relationship in your favour.

What's the alternative to self-love? Self-loathing? Self-pity? Self-hatred?

Seen in those terms it is obvious that self-love is the only possible choice.

*“Knowing others is intelligence.
Knowing yourself is true wisdom.
Mastering others is strength;
Mastering yourself is true power.”*

LAOZI

Five minute self-love exercise

Feel your body. Stroke your hair. Touch your face. Scan the length of your limbs. Deeply appreciate that this is your home and that it deserves to be treated with love and care.

Self-love questions to ask on a regular basis

1. What do I love doing alone?
2. What do I love doing with other people?
3. Who would I love to see tomorrow?
4. Who makes me laugh?
5. Where do I feel alive?
6. Where would I love to go next weekend?
7. Which feelings would I love to permeate my life?
8. Which emotions would I love to share with others?

By continually questioning ourselves about what, who and where we love, we help ensure that our attempts at self-love are honestly met.

QUOTES ARE TAKEN FROM

Aldous Huxley, 1894-1963, English writer

Alexander Pope, 1688–1744, English poet

Carl Jung, 1875–1961, Swiss psychiatrist

Charles de Gaulle, 1890–1970, French statesman

Charlotte Brontë, 1816–1855, English writer

Christian Bovee, 1820–1904, American writer

Coco Chanel, 1883–1971, French fashion designer

Eleanor Roosevelt, 1884–1962 diplomat, activist and First Lady of USA

Epictetus, c. 50–135AD, former slave and Stoic philosopher

Friedrich Nietzsche, 1844–1900, German philosopher

Gerard Manley Hopkins, 1844–1889, English poet

Johann Wolfgang von Goethe, 1749–1832, German polymath

Gustave Flaubert, 1821–1880, French writer

Heraclitus, c. 540BC–c. 480BC, Ancient Greek philosopher

Horace, 65–8BC, Roman poet

Jalāl al-Dīn Muhammad Rūmī, 1207–1273, Persian poet

Jane Austen, 1775–1817, English author

Jean de la Bruyere, 1645–1696, French philosopher

Jean-Jacques Rousseau, 1712–1778, French philosopher

John Lubbock, 1834–1913, English parliamentarian and writer

John Steinbeck, 1902–1968, American writer

Kipling, Rudyard, 1865–1936, English author of *The Jungle Book*

Laozi, 6th–5th century BC, Ancient Chinese founder of Taoism

Leo Tolstoy, 1828–1910, Russian author of *War and Peace*

Louisa May Alcott, 1832–1888, American writer

Lucy Maud Montgomery, 1874–1942, Canadian author of *Anne of Green Gables*

Mark Twain, 1835–1910 American writer

Omar Khayyam, 1048–1131, Persian polymath

Origen, 185–253, early Christian scholar

Oscar Wilde, 1854–1900, English writer

Plato, c. 428BC–c. 348BC, Ancient Greek philosopher

Plotinus, c. 204–270AD, Hellenistic metaphysical philosopher

Saint Augustine, 354–430, theologian

Samuel Smiles, 1812–1904, English writer

Socrates, 469–399BC, Greek philosopher

Viktor Frankl, 1905–1997, Austrian psychiatrist

Walt Whitman, 1819–1892, American writer

William Hazlitt, 1778–1830, English essayist

BIBLIOGRAPHY AND FURTHER READING

PS, I Love Me, Gina Swire, Panorama Press, 2021

A Woman's Self-Love, Victoria Burshtein, self-published, 2022

The School of Life, An Emotional Education, Alain de Botton, Penguin, 2020

Untamed, Glennon Doyle, Vermillion, 2020

The Oxford Dictionary of Quotations, Oxford University Press, 2004

The Oxford Book of English Verse, Oxford University Press, Christopher Ricks, 1999

USEFUL WEBSITES

theselfloveproject.com

theself-lovemovement.com

tinybuddha.com

nhs.org.uk

Managing Director Sarah Lavelle
Assistant Editor Sofie Shearman
Words Joanna Gray
Series Designer Emily Lapworth
Designer Katy Everett
Head of Production Stephen Lang
Production Controller Martina Georgieva

Published in 2023 by Quadrille, an imprint of Hardie Grant Publishing

Quadrille
52–54 Southwark Street
London SE1 1UN
quadrille.com

Cataloguing in Publication Data: a catalogue record for this book is available from the British Library.

ISBN 978 1 83783 051 0

Printed in China